Rockin'!
A Kid's Guide to Kinderdijke, Netherlands

Photography by John D. Weigand
Poetry by Penelope Dyan

Bellissima Publishing, LLC
Jamul, California
www.bellissimapublishing.com

Copyright © 2018 by Penny D. Weigand & John D. Weigand

All rights reserved. No part of this book may be
reproduced or transmitted in any form or by any means,
electronic or mechanical, including photocopying,
recording, or by any other means, or by any information or
storage retrieval system, without permission from the publisher.

ISBN 978-1-61477-335-1
First Edition

"Problem solving is a very good thing."

PENELOPE DYAN

Rockin'!
Bellissima Publishing, LLC

Introduction

If windmills weren't put here in Kinderdijke, then the entire place would have been a bog into which a man's boots would have simply sunk! Kinderdijke is unique. It tells the story of man against nature, seeking to carve out a place in a wet and boggy world! Dutch icons, built between 1739 and 1740, the polder mills are a step into the past. And two of the original mills can still be seen! During the nineteenth and twentieth centuries the mills were replaced with pumping stations; but in Kinderdijke, you can see how (for nearly one thousand years) these windmills battled the water. The Kinderdijke-Elshout complex (as it is known) was added to the UNESCO World Heritage list in 1997. And families still live in them!

Enjoy this 'learn to read' book written by the award winning author, attorney and former teacher, Penelope Dyan, with photographs by John D. Weigand. Marvel at the ingenuity of a people from times past. And when you are finished reading, you can go to Bellissimavideo's YouTube channel; and you can watch the free music video that goes along with this kid-sized book (with its extra large print) that fits perfectly in a kid-sized backpack! And you can see even more of Kinderdijke!

Rockin'!
Bellissima Publishing, LLC

Rockin'!
A Kid's Guide to Kinderdijke, Netherlands

Photography by John D. Weigand
Poetry by Penelope Dyan

You see two windmills.
They are sitting on top of a bank
of grass of the greenest green.
Their image creates a most
beautiful scene!

You see two more windmills.
One windmill seems close.
The other windmill seems far away.
(You are fascinated by this place.)
You ask your mother,
"How long can we stay?"

Ducks swim among the waterlilies.
And as the ducks swim past,
you try to hold on
to this moment in time;
because you want
this moment to last and last!

The very next thing that you see
is a VERY proud duck family,
a duck family of THREE!

Then you see some bright yellow
HUGE wooden shoes!
Behind them is a smaller shoe,
that perhaps a NORMAL sized person
(who is not a giant)
has actually worn AND used!
(You smile, and you wonder if that shoe
was lost by Cinderella,
or if perhaps this was a prince's shoe,
and was therefore lost by a fella!)

Next to a wooden swing,
in front of a windmill
you see many, many colorful flowers.
You imagine that the inhabitants
of this windmill,
just stop and rest here
for hours and hours!

Your eyes zoom in
to this green, white, blue and red
spoked wheel.
You are told that this
is the windmill's central control.
You decide this fact is important,
and that it is a quite interesting
fact to know!

There is something else to be seen.
A small yellow boat
sits among the waterlilies,
right between long grasses of green!

You see a black sheep.

The top of this windmill
shows its long ago building date.
You tell your mother,
"I want to see more!
And I just cannot wait!"

And as you see more and more,
you learn what these windmills
were intended for . . .
They were built with ingenuity
to remove the water from the land.
They were created by and through
a human mind and hand.
They were simply built
from what you are told,
(and as to what you now think)
so that into the wet bog
(long ago)
its inhabitants would NOT sink!

And as from this place
you all walk along,
Mom reminds you that each place
that you visit
has its own story, lesson and song.
"This place," your mom tells you,
"is about staying alive!
When torrents of water and rain came,
the people HAD to survive!"
You decide if the saying,
"Necessity is the mother of invention,"
is actually TRUE,
then the people of Kinderdijk,
did what they needed to do!

"It is always good and prudent to just use your head."

PENELOPE DYAN

www.ingramcontent.com/pod-product-compliance
Ingram Content Group UK Ltd.
Pitfield, Milton Keynes, MK11 3LW, UK
UKHW060134240426
12048UKWH00002B/37